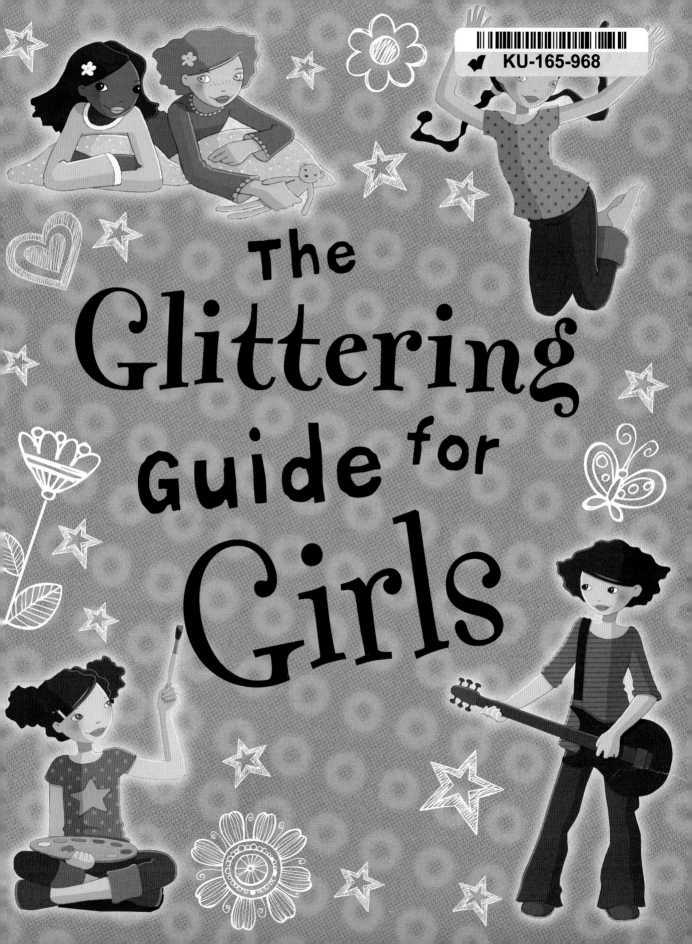

# The Glittering Guide for Girls

Editor: Mandy Archer
Designer: Nikki Kenwood
Illustrator: Jessica Secheret

Copyright © QED Publishing 2011

First published in the UK in 2011 by
QED Publishing
A Quarto Group company
226 City Road
London EC1V 2TT

www.qed-publishing.co.uk

A catalogue record for this book is available from the British Library.

ISBN 978 1 84835 791 4

Printed in China

**Picture credits**:
(t=top, b=bottom, l=left, r=right, c=centre, fc=front cover)
**Getty Images** 9t Steve Gorton and Karl Shone;
**iStockphoto** 9l kickers;
**Photolibrary** 12b Leanne Temme, 15t Ester Sorri, 103t Stockbrokerextra Images.
**Rex** 22l Image Source/Rex Features, 23r Burger/Phanie/Rex Features, 25tr Image Source/Rex Features, 25lc Design Pics Inc/Rex Features, 32r OJO Images/Rex Features; 66t OJO Images/Rex Features, 83b Burger/Phanie/Rex Features;
**Shutterstock** 8b wavebreakmedia ltd, 8 blue67design and azzzya (spot art), 10r R. Gino Santa Maria (girl on right), 10r Andresr (girl on left), 10b Christiana Mustion, 11b laola, 11b Bukhavets Mikhail (spot art), 13 Callahan (spot art), 13b Pinkcandy, 15c Elena Schweitzer, 16b Sparkling Moments Photography, 17b linnik, 18l ArrowStudio, LLC, 18b Dmitry Kolmakov, Coprid, Nika Novak, 19t a9photo, 19 Roslen Mack (spot art), 19l Zand, 20 Lavanda and nata_danilenko (spot art), 20r LittleRambo, 21l Ruth Black, 21c Mike Flippo, 21b Lev Dolgachov, 22 r c.byatt-norman, 23t sandra zuerlein and 1000 Words Images, 23 Elise Gravel (spot art), 24c liskus, 26b Fesus Robert, 27bl Huntstock.com, 27br stoyanh, 28l ArrowStudio, LLC, 29b Monkey Business Images, 30 PILart (spot art), 30b NinaMalyna, 31t clickthis (spot art), 31t saras66, 31tr Duncan de Young, 31r tatniz, 31c Alena Rozova, 31b Cre8tive Images, 33t Anke van Wyk, 36 blue67design and azzzya (spot art), 36t Ladyann, 36c Dmitry Kolmakov and jocic, 36b Karkas, zhu difeng and Evgeny Tyzhinov 37tr tracie andrews, cr clickthis, br aelitta, 37 asimjp (spot art), 38t Petro Feketa, 38tc HomeStudio, 38c Dmitry Kolmakov, 38r Teeratas, 39t Ragnarock, 40b Ilike, 41cl Alena Ozerova, 41cr Matthew Cole, 42t Ramona Kaulitzki, upstudio & malamalama, 42b Kiselev Andrey Valerevich, 43 Devor (spot art), 43b soloir, 44t Yuri Arcurs, 44c lanitta, 45t Olga Sapegina, 45b (annoyed tween) Sparkling Moments Photography, 46b nuttakit, 47t Cheryl Casey, 47c Kiselev Andrey Valerevich, 47b

M.antonis & kzww, 48c maximino, 48r Maksym Bondarchuk, 49t Anatema, 49cl Vojtech Beran, 50l elwynn, 50b Cosmin Munteanu, 51r Bluerain, 51b Aleksandar Mijatovic & Monkey Business Images, 52b Marish, 53l Eduard Titov, 53r Jules Studio, Beata Becla & Marilyn Volan, 53b terekhov igor, 54r iadams, 54b Felix Mizioznikov, 55 vladislav_studio (spot art), 55b Melianiaka Kanstantsin, 56 rusalo4ka (spot art), 56c bikeriderlondon, 57t Nicola Kenwood, 58r mixfree, 59r Mandy Godbehear, 59b Yuri Arcurs, 60 jagoda (spot art), 60bl New Image, 60br pandapaw, 61cl Juriah Mosin, 61r Imageman, 64 blue67design and azzzya (spot art), 64bl kavione and loriklaszlo, 65tr Valua Vitaly, 66c IQ Advertising, 66b CCallanan and val lawless, 67t Mandy Godbehear, 67cl S1001 and keellla, 67cr Miguel Angel Salinas Salinas, 68 Irina Nartova (spot arts), 68t Sparkling Moments Photography, 68b Juriah Mosin, 69b OJO Images/Rex Features and lavitrei, 70 Nowik (spot art), 70c Sandi67, 70b Jarp2, 71t 89studio, 71br Aleksandr Kurganov, 71bc Wolfe Larry, 73r Nikolay Moroz, 74t Poznyakov, 75r alexcoolok, 75b Ulrich Willmünder, 76b Piotr Marcinski, 77c Aleksandar Todorovic, 77b Tatiana Popova, Ton Lammerts, Picsfive, xjbxjhxm123, Tom Konestabo, 78b Alex Zabusik, 79cl Ladybuggy, 79cr Cheryl Casey, 80cr April Turner, 80cl deedl, 80cl cs333, 80br Catalin Petolea, 81t Ingvar Bjork, Creative Illus, John Kasawa, 82t Jack Qi, 84br Booka, 86b Monkey Business Images, 87c notkoo, 87r Andrey Klepikov, 87b Fernando Blanco Calzada, 88c Ariwasabi, 88b Dan Gerber, 89l Sergey Lazarev, 89c Miguel Angel Salinas Salinas, 92 blue67design and azzzya (spot art), 92l NatUlrich, 92r Alena Ozerova, 92b heromen30, 93l Elena Elisseeva, 93bc Anke van Wyk, 94r Diana Olsevska, 94 Stephanie Lirette (spot art), 94 khz (spot art), 95t Zand, 95l Alena Ozerova, 95b NatUlrich, 96 PILart (spot art), 96t Vibrant Image Studio, 96bl Angela Jones, 96br eAlisa, 97c Martin Mette, 97b Pete Saloutos, 98tl Amenhotepov, 98b Alexander Kalina, 99t Stawek, 99cl Olha Ukhal, 99cr FreeSoulProduction, 100 nata_danilenko (spot art), 100 Lota (spot art), 100c Yuri Arcurs,100b ifong, 101l Pilgrim Artworks, 101r Galayko Sergey, 101r Monkey Business Images, 101bl Kraska, 102t beboy, 102c Stephen Aaron Rees, 102b Monkey Business Images, 103c LittleRambo, 104 notkoo (spot art), 104t Rick P Lewis, 104b Booka, 105c Takra, 105b Gina Sanders, 106r Rakov Studio, 107t Yuri Arcurs, 107c Callahan, 107 Triling Studio LTd. (spot art), 108b zeljkosantrac, 108r zsooofija, 109tl U.P.images_vector, 109tr ildogesto, 109cl Shmeliova Natalia, 109br volod, 110tr Aleksandr Markin, 111r Ardelean Andreea, 111cl Yuri Arcurs, 111br maraga, 112t Monkey Business Images, 112c Monkey Business Images, 113t Liliya Kulianionak, 113b Fernando Blanco Calzada, 114t Pushkin, 114l Petro Feketa, 114lc Jiri Hera, 115 Lavanda and nata_danilenko (spot art), 115c Stavklem & Roman Kholodov, 115b michaeljung, 116t Monkey Business Images, 116t sonia.eps.

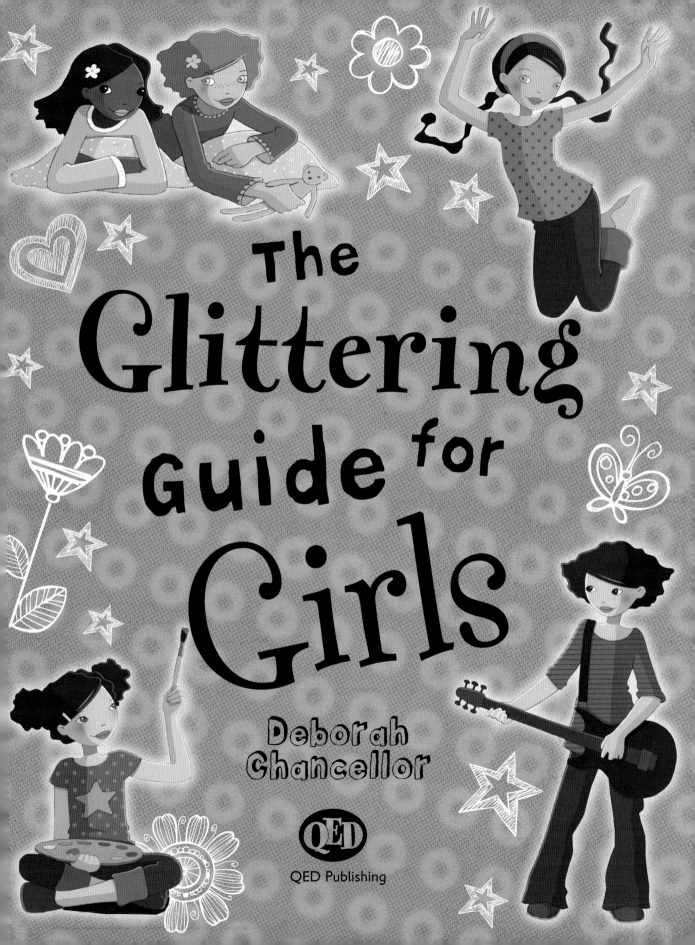

# The Glittering Guide for Girls

## Deborah Chancellor

QED

QED Publishing

# Contents

# Introduction

## Get ready for girl time!

From sleepover parties to friendship bracelets, the **Best Friends** section will help you make your friendships special.

**Cool Creative** is filled with imaginative projects – from bedrooom makeovers to scrapbooking, it's loaded with ideas for creative girls.

**Star Performer** is the perfect place for girls want their time to shine. Learn all about singing, dancing, acting and all your favourite performance arts.

Finally, answer all your questions about healthy living in **Happy and Healthy**. From sporty stuff and games to inner and outer beauty, fun ideas and helpful tips will make feeling good easy.

Best Friends

# Friends forever!

A best friend is a person to treasure. A true BFF (Best Friend Forever) is there to share the good times and the bad, ready to stand by you no matter what. Where would you be without your best friend?

## Sharing secrets

Best friends will listen to your secret hopes and dreams, as well as your worries. You must be able to trust your best friend not to tell a soul, and your best friend has to trust you, too!

## Keeping in touch

Friends love to talk all the time! There are tons of ways to keep in touch. Swap phone numbers or instant message a smiley face to your friend's PC. Texting is often cheaper than talking by phone – and just as much fun.

:) HAPPY
:( SAD
:O SHOCKED
:S CONFUSED
;) WINK
:D LAUGHING

## Special tokens

Exchange a gift with your best friend to show how much you care. You could even buy a special necklace with two matching halves. Keep one half each, so that every time you look at it you think of your best friend.

## Friendship bracelets

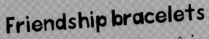

Learn how to weave friendship bracelets using knotted lengths of embroidery thread. Surprise your best friend by giving her a friendship bracelet made with her favourite colours.

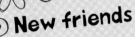

## Old friends

Having a new best friend can be so exciting, it's easy to forget about the rest of your pals. Try not to make your old friends feel left out – introduce them to your BFF and invite them on play-dates.

## New friends

Just because you have a best friend, it doesn't mean you can't make new friends, too! If your best friend doesn't like this, tell her how special she is and ask her to join in. Soon, you'll all be friends together!

# School's cool

School can be lots of fun – it's the perfect place to make friends and get to know them better. Work hard, but make the most of your playtimes too.

## Who's the new girl?

If a new girl arrives in your class, make an effort to talk to her. She is probably nervous and a bit shy. Introduce her to your friends and invite her to play with you at break time.

## Crazy crazes

What's the latest collecting craze at school? Perhaps it is stickers, key rings or gel pens. If your teacher won't let you bring collections into the playground, arrange swaps with your friends at home.

### Fun things to collect:

- magazines
- postcards
- buttons
- key rings
- gel pens
- stickers
- beads
- bookmarks
- hairclips

## Miss you!

It can be hard if someone you like moves away or changes schools. Take the plunge and try to make some new friendships. You can always keep in touch with your old friend, and she wouldn't want you missing her or feeling sad.

## Playground games

Long playtimes will flash by if you rope your crew into some playground games. Have you tried making up clapping rhymes that get faster and faster? Ask your teacher for some new ideas, or for help in agreeing the rules.

## Beat the bullies

If a person at school keeps saying and doing hurtful things to you, it can be very upsetting. If you think you are being bullied, talk to an adult you trust and they will help fix the problem.

## Samantha

Please come to my birthday party at Grove House, on Saturday at 6 o'clock.

Lots of love
Rachel xxxx

## Time for tact

If you're having an outing or a special tea and can only invite a few friends, don't hand out the invitations in front of everyone at school. It's a kind way of making sure the girls you can't invite don't feel left out.

# Who likes who?

Everyone wants to be popular, with friends queuing up for their attention! It can be easy to forget that quality is more important than quantity.

## Little Miss Popular

Some girls like being part of a big gang, while others are happy to hang out with one or two close friends. Both are good choices – we are all different, so different things make each of us happy.

## Look out for each other

To have a good friend you need to be a good friend. Take time to talk to your friend if she is upset and listen to her problems. Stick up for her and never make her worries seem silly.

## Top topics for starting friendships

Favourite movies, bands, books, clothes, school lessons, sweets.

## Make the first move

The best way to make friends is to be friendly! When you meet someone new, tell them your name and ask what they are called. Invite them to join in your game and chat while you play.

## Kindness counts

If you want your friends to like you, be thoughtful and don't say mean things behind their back. Relax and be yourself and they are sure to want to spend time with you.

## Be yourself

You don't have to copy everything that your friends say and do. Listen to your heart and stay true to yourself. The best friends are the people who accept you as you are, not the ones who want to change you.

## Good friends...

* listen as well as talk
* defend you every time
* never abandon a friend in need
* always make you smile!

## Fitting in

Do you ever feel under pressure to do something just because a friend told you to? If one of your pals is being bossy, find the courage to stand up to her. You might be surprised how many of your other friends are secretly feeling the same way!

13

# Forgive and forget

Arguments can erupt over the tiniest things! Don't let fights drag on – try and make up as soon as you can.

## Three's a crowd?

Sometimes it is hard for three friends to get along together. If two of you get super-close, the third person might feel left out. If this happens in your group of friends, talk about it. Things will get better if you explain how you feel.

## Copycats

Friends sometimes argue because one thinks the other is copying them. Remember that if your friend copies you, it is really because she likes you. Take it as a compliment and enjoy setting the trend!

## Gossip girl

If one of your friends discovers that you have said mean things about her, there's sure to be a bust-up. Before you fight back, take a moment to imagine how she must be feeling. Talk the problem over and you'll end up closer than before.

## Say sorry

After a fight, never be too proud to say sorry. Even if you didn't cause the argument, it's easy to say unkind things in the heat of the moment. If your friend apologizes to you, let her know that you forgive her.

## Making up is fun to do

Don't let an argument spoil a top friendship! Patch things up with a big hug, some kind words and a sparkly smile. If you really want to show your friend you are sorry, you could even give her a little present or write her a card.

Sorry

### Super "I'm sorry" gifts

- cupcakes
- nail varnish
- homemade jewellery
- a drawing or poem

## Put it behind you

Once you have made up with your friend, forget the argument ever happened. It is not fair to bring it up the next time that something goes wrong. Move on to the good times instead!

# Party time

A birthday is the perfect excuse to plan an unforgettable party for you and your friends.

## Who's coming?

First things first – find out how many people you can invite, then write a guest list. Try to pick pals who get on well together. If you leave out any of your best friends there could be trouble!

## Choose a theme

It's decision time. What kind of party do you want? If you love dressing up, choose a glam theme like 'Disco Divas'. If you'd prefer an active party, pick your favourite sport and ask your parents to book the venue.

## Design time

Design your party invitation on a laptop or PC. Choose a funky font for the words and paste in pictures to fit the theme. Don't forget to add all the vital information, such as the date, time and place!

## Setting the scene

Homemade decorations make a party extra special. Try painting banners and decorating balloons. You could even use photos of your friends to make place cards, so they know where to sit at the party table.

## Stand on your head for five seconds

## Sing a pop song like an opera star

## Giggles and games

When your friends arrive, rope them into some silly party games. Limbo dancing and musical bumps are great icebreakers, especially if you hand funny forfeits to your guests when they get caught out!

## Party playlist

You'll need music at your party, so make a playlist of your favourite songs on your MP3 player. Why not burn the playlist onto some CDs and pop them into party bags for your friends to take home at the end?

# Theme it!

Have you ever hosted a themed party? When your birthday comes round this year, try something a little different. Whether it's a beach barbecue, a masquerade disco or a pampering afternoon – the choice is up to you!

## Pop stars

If you're always singing along to pop songs, throw a karaoke party. Get a karaoke DVD or computer game, then invite your friends to come dressed as pop stars. The most dazzling outfit and performance get a prize!

## Crafty creations

If you and your friends love making things, collect some funky beads and craft materials for a jewellery making party. At the end of the festivities your guests will be able to take their fabulous creations home.

## Yummy pizza toppings

 olives and feta cheese
* chicken and mushroom
* pepperoni and chilli
* tuna and peppers

## Pizza parlour

Lay out some pizza bases and a selection of scrummy toppings, then invite your friends to decorate their meal before they eat it. Your pals will be flocking to your pizza party quicker than you can say 'Mamma mia'!

## Hop, flip, jump!

Ask your parents if you can host a super-springy trampoline party. A coach at your local sports centre will teach you and your friends some cool tricks, so you can all learn to bounce in style.

## Skate time

Roller- and ice-skating are fantastic fun! Invite your friends to a party in the park, or bop and glide at your nearest rink. Prepare for some tumbles before you get the hang of it! You might just discover a cool new hobby...

## Strike!

Anyone can try ten-pin bowling – beginners may discover a hidden talent and experienced bowlers can always improve their game. Split your friends into teams and let everyone choose a silly name. The team with the highest score could even get rosettes!

# Nibbles and treats

Getting ready for a party can be just as much fun as the celebration itself! Plan a few mouth-watering surprises and your big day is guaranteed to be a huge success.

## Make up a menu

Decide what kind of party food will tickle your friends' tastebuds. Remember to organize some vegetarian options for anyone who doesn't eat meat. If one of your guests has a food allergy, check that your choices are safe for her to eat.

## Make up a menu

cupcakes
chocolate-covered fruit
sausage rolls
mini pizzas
sandwiches
mini doughnuts
flapjacks
popcorn

## Celebration cake

Choosing the party cake is the birthday girl's privilege! If the cake is baked at home, help decorate it to match your party theme. Will you choose a tower of pretty pink cupcakes or a delicious chocolate gateau?

## Sweet surprise

A chocolate fountain is a special machine that melts chocolate for dipping at parties. Ask your parents to hire one for your birthday bash, then take turns dipping in marshmallows, strawberries and gingerbread shapes.

## Party piñata

A party piñata is a game and a treat all rolled into one! Buy or make one, then fill it with mini sweets and lollipops. Blindfold each other, then take turns to bash the piñata with a stick until the sweets scatter onto the floor!

## Going home time

At the end of your party, give your friends a pretty bag stuffed with gifts, balloons and sweets. Buy the bags in advance and put names on them so that nobody misses out. Don't forget to pop in a slice of party cake too!

**21**

# Essential sleepover kit

So you're going to a sleepover – be prepared! You'll have heaps more fun if you remember to take all the right things with you.

**Checklist:**
- ✔ PJs
- ✔ mobile phone
- ✔ toothbrush
- ✔ snacks
- ✔ clean clothes
- ✔ games console
- ✔ DVDs
- ✔ torch
- ✔ slippers

## Arrive in style

Make a good impression on your friends with a cool sleepover bag. Ask at home if you can have an old, small suitcase, then customize it with stickers and pictures of your favourite TV and pop stars.

Night, night!

## Mobile moments

Bring a mobile phone so you can take funny photos of your friends at the sleepover. Later on, you can also text home to say goodnight to your family.

## Fun and games

Don't forget to charge up your games console and pack it in your bag. If you have a favourite DVD, bring that along, too, so you can watch a midnight movie with your friends.

## Scrummy snacks

No sleepover would be complete without a proper midnight feast. Spend your pocket money on some pick 'n' mix to share in the middle of the night. Don't expect to bring any sweets home!

## Home comforts

Don't forget your toothbrush – you'll need to clean your teeth after all those sweets! Bring your own comfy pillow to help you to fall asleep – if your friends give you the chance, that is...

## Special cuddles

Last, but not least, don't leave home without your bedtime cuddly toy. He'll be lonely staying behind without you, and if you start to feel homesick at the sleepover, he will make you feel a lot better.

# Giggle the night away

The last thing you'll want to do at your sleepover is get much sleep! It's fun to stay up late with your friends, and there are all sorts of games that you can play to keep awake.

## Sooo spooky!
Flick off the light then switch on a torch. Huddle together and see who can tell the scariest ghost story. Don't scream too loudly or you'll wake up the neighbours!

## Wink murder
Choose a friend to be a 'detective' then send her out of the room. Decide who is to be the 'murderer', then call the detective back in. The murderer kills her victims by winking at them, one by one. Can your 'detective' catch the culprit in the act?

## Truth or dare?
When the rest of the household finally goes to bed, play this game with your friends. Toss a coin – if it's heads, tell a secret, and if it's tails, do something daring, like going downstairs in the dark all by yourself.

Get a nightmare makeover!

Swap clothes with the girl sitting next to you

## Movie marathon

Choose a bunch of films starring your favourite actor, then watch them all back-to-back! Who can stay awake until the final closing credits? Make a 'greatest fan' badge to present to the winner at breakfast-time!

## Camping out

In the summer, try hosting a camping sleepover. Put up a tent in your back garden, and ask your friends to bring torches, sleeping bags and warm pyjamas. Don't get spooked by all the night noises!

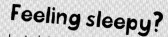

## Feeling sleepy?

Waking up the next morning won't be easy. Try not to doze off during the day, no matter how tired and grumpy you feel. Go to bed early the next night and you'll soon catch up on your missed beauty sleep!

# Sharing and swapping

Half the fun of having friends is that you can share and trade things with them. Clothes and cuddly toys that have been sitting in your cupboard for ages look new and exciting to someone else.

## Instant makeover

If you are the same size as your friend, you could do a clothes swap. It doesn't have to be permanent – you could just borrow something for a week. Check that your mum or dad is happy with the idea first.

## Cuddly exchange

Ask your friends to bring over a stuffed animal that they don't want any more. Put them in a pile and take it in turns to choose a 'new' toy to play with. Make a deal to meet in a month's time to have another swap around.

## Swap shop

There's no limit to the things you can swap! What about trading DVDs, accessories or magazines? It's best if you meet at a friend's house to do this and check at home before you give anything valuable away.

**Try swapping:**
DVDs, jewellery, CDs, books, shoes, hairclips, clothes, computer games.

## Give it away

At Christmas or on your birthday, you may get two of the same present. If this happens, don't sulk, but give your best friend the 'double'. Perhaps she'll share her presents with you next time.

## Bring and buy

Have a clear-out in your bedroom and persuade your friends to do the same. Meet up with your stuff and agree one fixed price for every item on sale. Take a little bit of cash and buy the things you fancy. Spend the profits on a group treat, or give the money to charity.

## Pamper parlour

Ask your friends to bring some make-up round to your house, so you can share it and try out new looks. Don't forget to take some 'before' and 'after' photos for a laugh!

# Chatting and blogging

There are lots of ways to connect to friends online – just be sure to check first that it's OK with your mum or dad.

## Online games

There are so many games that you can play online. Before you start, text your friends to ask if they are free to play too. You can even instant message while you play – just type something and wait for a reply!

## Text together

Texting is a great way to keep in touch. When you get a text, you know your friend is thinking about you! Always reply to your friend's texts or send her a smiley to show that you care.

## Chatting online

Social networking sites are really for teenagers and adults, but there are some special ones for pre-teens. Always ask a grown-up before logging on to new sites and be very careful about who you chat to.

## Get blogging

A blog is an online diary, where you type your thoughts and people reply. If you'd like to set one up ask your mum or dad to help you. Always show them your blog entries before you publish online.

## Cyber bullying

Chatting online is fun, but sometimes people can write messages that are unkind. This is called 'cyber bullying'. If anyone is nasty or rude to you online, tell your parents or a teacher so they can sort it out. Don't let the bully win.

## Keep it safe online

- **Don't** arrange to meet anyone you have only chatted to on the Internet.
- **Don't** give away your real name, birthday, address or phone number.
- **Don't** say where you go to school, or anything about your family.
- **Don't** post photos or information that could be used to hurt you or any of your friends.
- **Do** use strict security settings in chat rooms, so only friends you list can chat to you.

# Rainy day ideas

Do you dread getting stuck indoors on a rainy day? Grab some friends, then give one of these boredom-busting ideas a try!

## Terrific tresses

Set up a hair salon in your bathroom and start creating new hairstyles for your friends. Try high ponytails, loose buns and eye-catching plaits. Don't use scissors though – cutting is for the experts!

## Pamper yourselves!

Have a go at making luscious natural face masks. Try smearing on mashed avocado with a few drops of almond oil, or oatmeal mixed with natural yoghurt. Rest your eyes with slices of cool cucumber before you wash it all off!

## Nail bar

Tell your friends to bring their nail polish round to your place. Set up a nail station in the kitchen and paint each other's nails. Be creative – invent patterns, stick on gems and use lots of glossy colours.

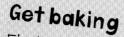

## Old-fashioned fun

Computer games are great, but sometimes it's fun to switch off the PC and go back to basics. Dig out your old board games from the cupboard, think up some crazy new rules, then challenge your friends to a match.

**Cookie flavours:** chocolate chips, marshmallows, peanuts, glacé cherries, coconut, lemon zest

## Get baking

Find a good, easy recipe for cookies and combine the ingredients. Follow the instructions and get baking! Which flavours will you stir in? Ask an adult for help when using the oven.

## Duck and dive

If it's wet outside, go swimming! It's a fantastic way to have fun and keep fit. The more friends you swim with, the better – so phone them all up and arrange a time to meet at your local pool.

31

# Out and about

The sun is shining, so don't sit around waiting for something exciting to happen! Grab your sunglasses and head outside.

## Check it out

Always let your mum and dad know what your plans are. Agree a time to get back and wear your watch so that you won't be late. Take your mobile phone and keep it switched on all the time.

## Retail therapy

Hit the shopping mall with a friend. Help each other to choose something stylish, like a bag, a necklace or a funky hair accessory. Don't worry if you both want to buy the same thing – maybe you could pretend to be twins!

## On your bike

If it's a long walk to your friends' place, cycle there, then go on a bike ride together. Check the route first at home to make sure it is safe – and don't forget to wear your bike helmet.

Other fun ways to get about:
- ★ go-karts
- ★ roller blades
- ★ skateboards
- ★ scooters

## Secret den

Make a den at the bottom of your garden or ask your parents to take you to the park. Find a tree with low branches and hang an old rug over them. Take cushions to sit on and snacks to eat inside your den.

## Safe spot

Always play in safe places with your friends. Never hang out near a railway track or busy road. Stay away from building sites and deserted spots. If you're not sure about a place, don't go and play there.

## Stranger danger

When you are out, remember the golden rule – never talk to strangers. Keep on walking even if the person is friendly and offers you presents or sweets. Never accept a lift from someone you don't know very well.

# Best friends' quiz

What sort of best friend are you? Find out the answer in this special friendship quiz.

1. **How do you keep your best friend happy?**
   a   never make any new friends
   b   ignore all your old friends
   c   keep your best friend's secrets

2. **What is the best way to make friends?**
   a   buy people presents
   b   talk and listen to people
   c   wear the same clothes as everyone else

3. **How do you make up after an argument?**
   a   say sorry and hug your friend
   b   tell your friend she was wrong
   c   never forget what happened

4. **How do you decide on your party list?**
   a   invite everyone so you get lots of presents
   b   choose friends who get on well together
   c   pick the most popular girls

5. **How do you choose party food?**
   a   choose all your favourite snacks
   b   leave all the decisions to someone else
   c   make sure there is a variety of food

6. **What should you do if you take your favourite sweets to a sleepover?**
   a   save yours and eat all your friends' sweets
   b   share them with all your friends
   c   let your friends eat some, but save most for yourself

7. **What do you do if your friend texts you?**
   a   ignore it
   b   wait a few days then reply
   c   reply as soon as you can

8. **Your friend asks you to give her a new hairstyle. What do you do?**
   a   agree to the idea - if she does your hair afterwards
   b   cut her hair short
   c   refuse to touch her hair

*Look back at these pages: Friends forever! (pages 8-9); Who likes who? (pages 12-13); Forgive and forget (pages 14-15); Party time (pages 16-17); Nibbles and treats (pages 20-21); Essential sleepover kit (pages 22-23); Chatting and blogging (pages 28-29); Rainy day ideas (pages 30-31).*

## How well did you do? Count your correct answers below to find out!

0-3   You're on the right track, but there's lots more to learn about being a good friend and staying true to yourself.

4-6   Pretty good! You are great at meeting new people and being pals with the friends that you've got.

7-8   You're the best! Most girls would love a friend like you - keep up the good work!

Quiz answers: 1. c; 2. b; 3. a; 4. b; 5. c; 6. b; 7. c; 8. a

Cool Creative

# New you

Pop stars and celebs are always changing the way they look – why not you? Here's how to give yourself a makeover without spending a fortune.

## Jazzy jeans

Dig out your old jeans and get creative! Sew on patches, badges and bows. Copy the designer look by ripping or snipping the denim in places. You could even cut your jeans into cool shorts.

## Trend setter

Don't moan about your old, plain T-shirts – use special fabric paints or pens to give them a brand-new look. Remember to practise your designs on paper first.

## Boho bag

If you've grown out of your favourite jeans, transform them into something new. Cut off the legs and sew the leg holes together to make a bag. Tie the ends of a silky scarf on to two belt hoops and you'll have a pretty strap.

## Busy badges

Pin badges are a great way to stand out from the crowd. Most craft shops sell brilliant badge kits, or you could find some card, sticky-back plastic and safety pins, then have a go yourself.

## Designer details

- ♡ ribbons
- ♡ fabric pens
- ♡ lace
- ♡ buttons
- ♡ brooches
- ♡ sequins and sew-on gems

## Mix 'n' match

Customize old hair accessories to set off a brand-new outfit. Try sticking sparkly jewels on to hair clips, or sewing pretty coloured sequins onto a scrunchie. Trimmed scarves and ribbons look fab too.

## Customizing kit

Before you throw anything away, see if there is any part of it that can be saved and stitched into something new. Keep buttons, patches and cute trims in a special bag – ready for you to rummage in next time you are feeling artistic.

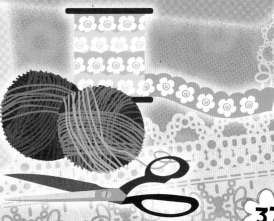

# Bangles and boxes

Do you have trouble finding room for all your treasures and trinkets? Declutter your dressing table then make some cute new pieces to display!

## Beauty box

Make a home for your hair accessories. Cover a shoe box with stickers and photos from glossy magazines. Cut up some thick card and fit it snugly inside the box to make sections for clips, Alice bands, ribbons and hair jewellery.

## Get personal

Make a feature out of personalizing your things – they'll be so much harder to lose! Use enamel paints to decorate a plain, plastic Alice band with your name, using all of your favourite colours.

## Treasure trove

If you fancy a trendy new jewellery box, just revamp your old one! Stick on some cool collage materials. Use strong craft glue, so that your decorations don't fall off.

## Brilliant bangles

Bangles can take up loads of space in your jewellery box. Use nail polish to paint a blank CD holder in rainbow colours. Now you've got the perfect home for all your chunky wristbands!

## Top 10 pretty things

1. holofoil paper
2. sweet wrappers
3. beads
4. fabric scraps
5. coins
6. shells
7. tassels
8. feathers
9. confetti
10. pressed flowers

## Make Mum's day

Glass beads are fun to collect, and they also make beautiful necklaces and bracelets. Thread a matching set in your mum's favourite colours then present it to her as a gorgeous thank-you gift.

## Special gift

If you want to make a special gift for your best buddy, try creating a paper bead necklace. Cut out thin triangular strips from colourful magazines, then tightly wind each strip around a drinking straw. Cover with clear glue and leave to dry, then cut up and thread!

# Makeover madness

Is your bedroom lacking some va va voom? With a bit of effort and a few pots of paint, you can transform it into the perfect personal pad.

## Make some space

It's hard to be creative if there is too much clutter around you. Set aside one Saturday to have a thorough clear-out, then take all your unwanted toys, books and clothes to a charity shop.

## Colour change

Ask your mum or dad if you can paint your room a new colour. Think carefully about the shade you like – the colour will set the mood for the whole space.

## All change

You can make your room seem bigger by moving furniture around. Draw a plan of your room, showing where you want everything to go. Check with your parents before you shift the big items.

## Tidy up

If you've got loads of stuff, you'll need to find places to put it all. Grab some boxes and paint them in contrasting colours to your walls. Fill the boxes with your things and store them under your bed or desk.

## Soft landing

Cushions and beanbags make your room extra comfy and create a relaxed atmosphere. Give your old cushions a makeover by sewing on pretty patches, or making funky fur covers.

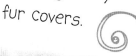

## Girls allowed!

Your bedroom's not complete without your own special door sign. Try designing one on your computer – make your name stand out with a funky font style. Now laminate your sign and hang it up!

### Keep out!
#### Emma's room

Colours to match your mood

pink    cosy and comfy

blue    cool and quiet

lilac    relaxing and soothing

green    calm and peaceful

yellow    sunny and cheerful

orange    friendly and bold

# Hot collections

Are you crazy about collecting? It's fun to build up a special box of treasures to show to your friends. Maybe you'll start a trend...

## Collector club
Find out if there is a website or magazine that will tell you more about the kind of object you like to collect. The more that you learn, the bigger and better your collection will become.

## Get this!
Want to start a new collection, but not sure what to go for? Here are some items that will look fantastic when displayed on any bedroom shelf.

- snow globes
- key-rings
- fridge magnets
- animal figurines
- costume dolls
- crystals
- fossils

## On show
Don't hide your collection away! Ask an adult to put up some shelves for you. Make sure there will be enough space to display your collection, plus some room to spare as it grows!

## Top trades

When you begin a sticker or card collection, check if some of your pals are collecting the same thing. That way, when you get doubles, you can arrange to do swaps.

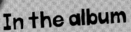

## In the album

A clever trading tip is to make up two albums. Use one for your collection, and the other for doubles. Keep your collection at home, and bring the doubles out with you to swap with friends.

## Complete collection

If you manage to complete a whole series of cards or stickers, keep them safe in your album. One day, your collection will bring back happy memories and it may even be worth a fortune!

# Secret diary

Do you write a diary, or are you thinking about starting one? Here are some secrets to help you create the most exciting journal ever!

## Dear diary

Be realistic about the amount you can write. Find a time to write that works for you, when you're not too busy or tired. If you write in it at the same time each day, it will become a habit that you won't forget.

## Book it in

Find a hardback notebook to write in. You could buy a diary with a lock, but take care not to lose the key or forget the combination. Customize the cover with patterns and doodles of your favourite things.

My Diary

## What to write?

Write about the interesting stuff that happens to you and leave out all the boring bits. Don't go into detail about what you had for lunch or your lessons at school. Instead, dish out the day's juicy gossip and describe the funniest moments!

## Hands off!

The most thrilling thing about your diary is keeping it secret. Keep an eye on any pesky brothers or sisters – don't let them get their hands on it!

## Hiding places

Swap your hiding places around, but don't forget where you've put your diary for the next time you want to make an entry!

### Good places
✔ behind your book shelf
✔ in your sock drawer
✔ under the mattress

### Bad places
✗ in your bed
✗ in your school bag
✗ on your desk

## Busted!

What if someone reads your diary? If you've written some upsetting stuff about them, say you are sorry, but remind the person that they shouldn't have read your private diary in the first place.

# Clever codes

Try writing your diary in code, so no one else can read it. Remember how to crack your code, or you won't be able to understand all the brilliant stuff you've written afterwards!

### 3-shift cipher

Write out the alphabet, and then write it again in capital letters on the line below 3 spaces over. Your two lines should look like this:

| a | b | c | d | e | f | g | h | i | j | k | l | m | n | o | p | q | r | s | t | u | v | w | x | y | z |
|---|---|---|---|---|---|---|---|---|---|---|---|---|---|---|---|---|---|---|---|---|---|---|---|---|---|
| X | Y | Z | A | B | C | D | E | F | G | H | I | J | K | L | M | N | O | P | Q | R | S | T | U | V | W |

With this code, the alphabet gets shifted along by three spaces. You write 'X' instead of an 'a', 'Y' instead of a 'b' and so on. If you want to write 'bad', put down 'YXA'.

### Fake names

Writing in code takes up lots of time. If you're in a hurry, then you could just write special names and places in code. Otherwise try choosing fake names for the people you are writing about.

Code message =
PQLM OBXAFKD
JV AFXOV!

Translated message =
Stop reading my diary!

46

## Amazing anagrams

Disguise people's names by turning them into anagrams. Use the same letters, but put them in a different order. For example, the name 'Catherine' could become 'A rich teen'.

## Back to basics

Write things backwards to confuse people who are trying to sneak a peek at your diary. 'Don't be nosy' looks much more baffling written as 'yson eb tnod'. Don't try this trick too often or it will be easy to spot.

## Hidden messages

Hide the words you want to write in a sentence, so they only appear every sixth word. For example, 'My Mum really loves my little brother when he says her perfume smells nice' hides the words 'My brother smells'.

## Invisible ink

Ever used invisible ink in your diary? Write something with a cotton wool bud dipped in lemon juice. To see what you have written, shine a bright torch on to the page.

# Snap happy

Taking photos is great fun and it's so easy. You don't need a big expensive camera – just start clicking away with your mobile phone!

## Camera crazy

If you're turning into a keen photographer, ask for a digital camera for your birthday or borrow one from your mum or dad. Take as many photos as you like, then delete the ones you don't want to keep.

## Time to text

Text your photos to your mates to cheer them up or share a giggle. Sometimes the funniest pics are the out-takes – the ones that didn't turn out quite as you planned...

## Photo opportunity

Many mobiles, hand-held game consoles and MP3s have cameras built into them. Learn how to use the photo function and practise taking pics at your next sleepover!

## Look again

Think carefully about the kind of photos you enjoy snapping and keep an eye out for unusual subjects. Try capturing something ordinary from a brand-new angle.

## Photo portfolio

- pretty portraits
- landscapes
- party pictures
- action shots
- animal magic
- city scenes

## Photo booth

Meet your pals at the shops then pile into a photo booth – how many of you can fit in? Strike funny poses, then cut up the strip so everyone gets to take a picture home with them.

## Save and send

Learn how to upload your photos onto a computer so that you avoid using up the memory disk on your phone or camera. Once you've got your pics stored on your computer, you can start emailing them to friends and family.

# Smile!

Do you love taking photos, but sometimes feel disappointed with the results? Don't give up – there are all sorts of ways to improve your technique.

## In the picture

Be careful how you frame your shot. If you are snapping people, don't stand too far away. For a great photo, think about what's close to you, as well as what's in the distance. Try turning your camera sideways to see if a vertical shot looks more interesting.

## Ready, steady, go…

To take great action shots, use a camera with a fast shutter speed. If you don't want any blurring, you'll need to hold it perfectly still. It might help to fix the camera on to a mini-tripod.

## Gotcha!

The best photo opportunities happen when you are least expecting them. Be ready, so if you see something you want to photograph, you won't miss it. Always have your camera handy!

## Lights, camera, action!

Check that there's enough light to take your photo and make sure there are no shadows going over your subject. Look at the angle that the light is coming from, and don't face the sun when taking your shot.

## How cute!

If you want to take animal photos, start with your pet. Take lots of pics so he or she gets used to the camera, then try to capture their personality with a few close-ups. You'll bag the best shots if you get down on their level.

## Fab photo checklist

- ❏ Are you close enough to your subject?
- ❏ Have you sussed out what's in the background?
- ❏ Have you included all your subject in the frame?
- ❏ Do you need to use a flash?
- ❏ Do your fingers cover the lens?

## Red eye

Do the people in your photos sometimes end up with glowing red eyes? This can happen when the flash shines into their eyes. Some computer programs can fix this problem before you print the photos out.

51

# Photo gallery

Pictures are made for sharing – so don't hide them away! There are all kinds of creative ways to display the special moments that you've captured.

## Photo board

Get a pin board for your room then put up photos of all your favourite people and animals. Add some silly speech bubbles to make your friends laugh! Change your montage as often as you wish.

## Perfect present

Digital photo companies can print your shots on to anything from mugs to mouse mats. You could also use your pics to personalize a calendar for your family.

## Photos dazzle ...

- as screen savers
- in collages
- on birthday cards
- in key-rings
- on the fridge
- in photo frames

## Funky frames

Customized photo frames are perfect for those extra-special pictures. Add glamour to a plain wooden frame by sticking on feathers, glitter and sequins. Now it's ready to display a happy photo of you and all your friends!

## Amazing albums

The best way to organize your pictures is to sort them into albums. It's easy to forget when and where you took a photo, so write a caption and date next to each one.

## Simply the best?

If you've got stacks of similar photos, don't put them all together in your album – just choose the best of the bunch. You could slip in a few embarrassing out-takes for a laugh!

## Protect your pics

Don't leave your photos in your phone or on your computer – if you upgrade you could lose them all. Print out your favourite pictures, then back them up by saving a copy on to a CD.

# Super scrapbooks

Why not get creative and start scrapbooking? You'll get stunning results with just a few simple craft materials and a sprinkling of imagination!

## Pick a theme

Choose a theme for a page in your scrapbook, such as your summer holiday. Collect photos, keepsakes and collage materials to go with your theme.

## Time to choose

Crop the photos you want to use, or overlap them for a montage effect. Be selective, because you may only have room for one or two shots on a page.

## Sticky business

Don't stick anything down until you are happy with the layout of your page. Use good craft glue that dries clear, and make sure that everything is well fixed. Don't shut the scrapbook until the glue is dry!

## Cool collage

Lay out everything you want on the page, starting with the background material. Add layers of photos and mementoes to build up an eye-catching collage. Leave enough space to write some captions.

SUMMER
fun
in the
sun
DAYS

## Caption time

Ask for help remembering interesting facts and stories to record in your scrapbook. Describe funny moments or write down special quotes. If you type your captions, pick interesting fonts and colours.

### Essential scrapbooking kit

- ♡ Souvenirs and keepsakes
- ♡ Fabric scraps
- ♡ Coloured sheets of card
- ♡ Textured papers and tissue
- ♡ Pretty stickers
- ♡ Glitter
- ♡ Gel pens

# Brilliant books

Now you've got the hang of scrapbooking, you've got the skills to create all sorts of wonderful journals that everyone will want to share.

## Cover story

The front cover of your book should give you a taste of what's inside. Write the title in big decorative letters, then draw pictures around the edge or create a bright collage border.

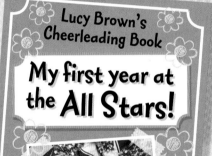

Lucy Brown's Cheerleading Book

My first year at the All Stars!

## Twelve top months

Find a large scrapbook, then create a fascinating record of the year according to you! Every month you could stick in seasonal photos, amazing news stories and souvenirs from the parties and days out that you enjoyed.

## School days

Collect your best school pics, and save programmes and newsletters too. Start a school scrapbook to share with your mates – it's funny to see how you have all changed during the year! Don't forget to write in everybody's names.

Coming home from hospital

Me aged 3

My 5th birthday

## This is my life

Ask your family to dig out pictures of you as a baby, a toddler and as a little girl. Make a special album that's all about you, writing the age you were underneath each of the photos. Include lots of facts and stories too.

## Momentous milestones

⭐ First tooth
⭐ First steps
⭐ Riding a bike
⭐ First day at school
⭐ Birthdays
⭐ Christmas

## Stencil it

Stencilling is a great way to decorate your scrapbooks. You can buy plastic stencils from craft shops, or ask an adult to cut your own design out of a thick sheet of card. Just lay your stencil down, then dab paint on it with a piece of sponge.

## Keep it clean

When you've finished your scrapbook, take the time to carefully laminate the cover with sticky-back plastic. The plastic will stop it from getting marked or creased.

# Gorgeous greetings

Home-made cards are so much better than shop-bought ones. A design by you shows how much you really care about your friends and family.

## Getting started

Grab some felt-tipped pens and your art supplies, plus some rough paper for doodling. Sketch a few ideas first, then transfer your favourite one onto a folded piece of white card. Colour in your design and stick on pretty decorations.

## Inside and out!

Make sure your envelope looks stunning by covering it with flourishes and patterns. Try designing your own pretend postage stamp in the top corner!
Inside the card use your best handwriting for the message.

## Rhyme time

Why not compose a short poem to go inside your card? Try to make it rhyme if you can!
Write the poem by hand, or type and print it so you can stick it in the right place.

Dear Amy,
The time has come to send to you
Special hugs and kisses too.
This little card is just to say,

Have a super 10TH BIRTHDAY!

Jade xoxoxo

## Pop-up surprise

Ask an adult to help you make a simple pop-up card using two sheets of paper. A pair of cut-out triangles folded back on the first sheet then pasted onto an outer sheet will look like a moving mouth when the card is opened up.

## Pretty pad

You could use your craft materials to decorate other things too! Why not customize a special notebook or diary? You could give it to your pal for her next birthday.

42 Smithson Avenue, Huckleberry, Peterston PT2 8HG

## Neat notepaper

Design some personalized notepaper on your computer. Use a pretty font to type your address at the top of the page, then decorate the notepaper with some clip art.

# Great gifts

Gifts you create yourself are special because they are completely unique! Each present is a designer one-off that is sure to be kept forever.

## Mum's mirror

Make a special mirror for your mum. Cover the frame with a layer of soft clay, then press in seashells to make a pattern. It's the perfect way to use those shells you collected last summer!

## Stuck on you

Why not make a fridge magnet for your grandparents? Get some polymer clay and a small magnet. Make a model of a cute animal, like a hedgehog, press the magnet underneath and leave it to set.

## What a mug!

Get a plain white mug and paint on some funky stripes with enamel paints. If this is a gift for your dad, you could also personalize the mug with his name.

Daddy Monty

## The sky's the limit

The Internet and your local library are both great sources for craft ideas. Birthdays are the ideal time to try out some brand new projects to give to your friends and family.

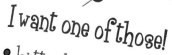

## Tidy up!

Make your brother or sister a desk tidy. Cut some cardboard tubes to different lengths and fix them onto a small shoebox lid. Decorate the desk tidy with colourful acrylic paint.

## Just charming

Design a phone charm for your best friend to remind her to call you! Buy some alphabet beads from a craft shop, threading them together to spell out her name.

# Cool creative quiz

Are you smart about art? See how you rate in the arty stakes in this cool creative quiz.

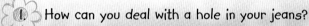

**1.** How can you deal with a hole in your jeans?
- a   throw them away and get a new pair
- b   cover up the hole with a funky patch
- c   tear more holes to get a designer look

**2.** None of your clothes match. What do you do?
- a   wear them anyway and hope no one notices
- b   swap some of your clothes with a friend
- c   customize them to make them match

**3.** Where do you store your bits and bobs?
- a   in decorated boxes
- b   stuffed under your bed or in a drawer
- c   they just get thrown away

**4.** What do you if you're bored with your bedroom?
- a   nothing – it's too much effort to change it
- b   swap rooms with your brother or sister
- c   re-arrange the furniture and paint your room a new colour

**5.** How do you react when your pal starts a key-ring collection?
- a   start your own collection of a favourite thing
- b   copy her and start collecting key-rings too
- c   tell her it's a silly idea

**6.** What's the best way to start writing a diary?
- a   buy a pretty notebook
- b   find a good time to write every day, so it becomes a habit
- c   write an essay as your first entry

**7.** How do you improve your photography?
- a   experiment with different techniques
- b   blame your camera and give up
- c   keep trying, but don't show anyone your pics

**8.** What sort of card do you give a friend?
- a   a bought one; life's too short to make one
- b   you make a card, but you'll only give it if it looks 100 per cent professional
- c   you make a card because it shows how much you care

Look back at these pages: New you (pages 36-37); Bangles and boxes (pages 38-39); Makeover madnes (pages 40-41); Hot collections (pages 42-43); Secret diary (pages 44-45); Snap happy (pages 48-49); Smile! (pages 50-51); Gorgeous greetings (pages 58-59).

## How well did you do? Count your correct answers below to find out!

**0-3**   You like the idea of being creative, so do something arty today! It's well worth the effort.

**4-6**   You do have flair, but don't always make your ideas happen. Be more confident and your mistakes will turn into masterpieces!

**7-8**   You're bursting with creative ideas. Once you start, there's no stopping you!

**62**

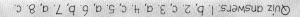
Quiz answers: 1. b, 2. c, 3. a, 4. c, 5. a, 6. b, 7. a, 8. c.

Star Performer

# Sing up!

It's easy to show off your musical talent – just open your mouth and sing! Singing every day is very good for you and will always put you in a happy mood.

## Getting started

The most talented singers treat their voices like precious musical instruments. Warm up gently, don't strain as you sing and remember to practise regularly. Even ten minutes a day will make a big difference!

## Private practice

Until you get the hang of it, you might prefer to practise on your own. Try singing in front of the mirror, using the hairbrush as a microphone! Take deep, even breaths so that you can hold the long notes for just the right time.

## Look and learn

Flick on your favourite music channel, then watch how the celebs sing their songs. Now join in, carefully copying their vocal style. If you can't remember all the lyrics, scribble them down in a notebook.

## Listen to me!

Top singers need an audience! If your pals won't listen to you, perform for your family. Pick a time when they're not too busy so they can give you an honest reaction. If all else fails, try serenading your pet!

## Join forces

Once you've got the basics, you're ready to start singing with a group of friends. Find a song you all know inside out, then have a go at singing it a capella – this is a musical term for performing a song without any instruments!

## Learn the ropes

To be the best, you'll need expert help. Every top singer has a teacher! When your next birthday comes round, ask your mum or dad if you can have singing lessons. If there's a choir or music club at school, sign up! It's a great place to improve your vocal skills.

## Audition tips

- choose a song to suit your voice
- practise for the audition
- stand up straight
- flash a big smile
- introduce yourself
- project your voice clearly
- if you make a mistake, keep going!

# Karaoke star

Do you long to be a pop star, packing stadiums with crowds of adoring fans? Grab a mike, put on your favourite tune, then start singing!

## What is karaoke?

Karaoke is a fab pastime that started in Japan. It means performing your favourite songs to backing tracks. If you practise with a video or computer game, the lyrics come up on screen as you sing.

## Word perfect

Choose a hit that you can rock out to, then memorize the words. Once you've done this, you'll be free to concentrate on your dazzling performance rather than just getting the lyrics right.

## Look the part

When you've finished practising, it's time to add a little sparkle! Dressing like a pop star can make you feel more confident – and this helps you to sing better. Before you perform a karaoke number for your pals, give yourself a cool celebrity makeover!

Rock star accessories
- ☆ cool shades
- ☆ hair jewels
- ☆ neon tights
- ☆ bling rings
- ☆ body glitter

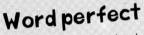

## Girl power

If you feel a little shy about taking the mike, ask your friends to join in too. There are so many amazing girl groups that you could sing along to. Work out a dance routine and split up the lines so that you all get to take equal turns.

## Show the world

When you're happy with your karaoke performance, get a friend to camcord you. Download the movie, grab some snacks, then relax and enjoy the show – there's bound to be loads of giggles as you watch yourselves on screen!

## Karaoke sleepover

If your friends are as karaoke crazy as you, invite them to a special singing sleepover. Put invites in CD cases and ask your guests to come dressed as pop divas ready for a late-night show!

# Smash hit

You're mad about music, so why not try composing a brand-new hit? Follow these song-writing tips and one day you could be number one in the downloads chart!

## Remix

Composing can be daunting at first, so begin by writing new words to a song that you know already. Match your words to the mood of the tune – whether the track is sad, happy or buzzing with energy.

## Write a rhyme

Listen again to the original song, then try to make your new words rhyme in the same places. That's not always as easy as it sounds! It might help to break the verses down line-by-line and practise singing new lyrics out loud.

## Songbird

Now you're ready to compose a brand-new song of your own. Begin with the words – write a short poem about something that makes you laugh or cry. Repeat two or three of the best lines to make a chorus.

## Melody maker

Think about the spirit of your poem. Is it sassy, sorrowful or sweet? Hum notes or experiment with a keyboard until you come up with a melody that suits this mood, repeating a section of it for the chorus or 'bridge'.

## Two become one

It's time to put your words and melody together! Don't panic if you don't know how to read or write music. Record your song, then play it to someone who can write the notation down on paper for you.

**Funky song themes**
- girl power
- feeling blue
- party party
- I miss you
- in my dreams

## Première performance

Work and rework your song, pouring your heart and soul into every note. Video yourself as you perform, trying out any new ideas that might make it better. When you're ready, perform it for your friends and family. Tell them it's a world première!

# Dancing feet

Do you get lost in music every time you step on to the dance floor? You're just the person to come up with a sizzling new routine!

## Star turns

Before you try and choreograph a routine from scratch, take a look at how the professionals do it. Watch your fave divas perform on TV, then practise their signature moves in front of a mirror.

## Making moves

Choose a song to dance to. Listen to the lyrics, then invent a set of eight steps that fit well with the music. Think about movements that will bring the song to life. Keep the moves simple so that you don't miss a beat.

## No limits

Don't forget that you can mix different styles of dance together in the same performance. If you like ballet, ballroom or tap, try incorporating some of those steps into your routine.

## Never forget

As soon as you stop dancing, record the moves you've built into your routine so far – it would be a shame to forget anything! Write all the steps down or invent symbols to stand for the different moves.

clap hands

twirl

side step

shimmy

## Pass it on

Teach your pals the new dance routine. Don't expect them to pick it all up straight away. Make sure they learn each section off by heart before you go on to teach some more.

## Strike a pose

Before you wow your audience with a performance, decide what poses you and your dance troupe want to hold at the start and end of the song. This will add stacks of attitude and atmosphere to your routine!

# You've got talent!

Putting on a talent show is a great way to get yourself and your pals up on stage! Recruit an organizing committee, then ask if you can host it at school. You'll have fun – and raise money for charity too.

## Tell the world

Make posters on your computer and stick them up all round school, so everyone knows when the show is happening. Make it clear that contestants can entertain the audience in any way they like – singing, dancing, telling jokes or doing magic tricks!

## Circle the date

Ask your teacher to agree the date and time for the talent contest. Make it an evening so all your families and friends can come along. They may want to get on stage and perform too!

**MAY 18**

## Poster checklist
- Date
- Time
- Place
- Entry cost
- Name of charity

### CALLING ALL RISING STARS!

**TALENT SHOW**

In the school hall
At 7pm on
Saturday 18th May
Tickets £1

All proceeds to the school charity

## Get your act together

So what about you? Do you want to enter the talent contest by yourself, as a solo act, or as part of a larger group? Don't let organizing the event stop you from showcasing your special talent too!

## Casting call

Sign your mates up for the contest – and your family too! Perhaps your little brother is a whizz at impressions or your best friend is brilliant at playing the violin. Find out what everyone's hidden talents are, then persuade them to show off to an audience.

## Try, try and try again

Learn your act, and rehearse it properly. Whatever you do, don't leave everything to the last minute. Try and work in a few surprises to make the audience remember you at voting time.

## And the winner is...

Pick three people to be judges at the talent contest. Get the audience to vote on the winner, just like they do on TV. You could even make signs for the judges to hold in the air!

# Tall tales

Are you a budding writer? Authors and playwrights get to share their ideas with readers all over the world! Use these tricks of the trade to improve your own unique writing style.

## Bookworm

The best writers have always got their nose in a book. When you read a story, you can learn for yourself what works well on the page. Reading helps you discover what kind of writer you want to be.

## Different stories

When you're ready to start writing, you need to decide what kind of story to tell. Think about the books you like reading and the subjects that you know a lot about. Maybe you're really into horses, or you had an amazing holiday that gave you a great setting for a new tale?

## Plan it out

All stories need a clear beginning, middle and end. Before you start, plan out the plot in a one-page summary, or synopsis. Grab your reader's attention, develop the action, then invent a nail-biting surprise finish.

### Six of the best

1. Real-life drama
2. Comedy
3. Ghosts and ghouls
4. Historical adventure
5. Fantasy and magic
6. Science fiction

## Cast list

Great stories feature memorable characters that leap off the page. Decide who they'll be and imagine how they'd talk to each other. What are their names? Help your reader really get to know the characters by including lots of speech in your story.

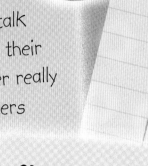

## Check it over

Every writer needs to go back to add extra details and make corrections. When you finish writing a story, you haven't really finished! Read through what you have written and make changes if you need to.

## Key change

Learn to type – you can pick up this skill by practising on your PC or laptop. Handwrite your story then type it up, so that you can make changes or add extra descriptions as you go.

# Read out loud!

There's nothing like a good yarn. If you want to write well, story-telling is a super way of developing your creative skills. Invite an audience to gather round, then lead them into the world of your imagination...

## A story to tell

If you've written a story that you're proud of, don't hide it away – share it! Practise putting on voices for the different characters and run through any tricky words so that you're not caught out during the reading.

## Test it out

When you rehearse, try speaking in front of a mirror – that way you can experiment with gestures and faces that will bring the story to life. If you've got a younger brother or sister, tell your story to them. See which bits they like, or find boring.

## On the edge of your seat

As you tell your story, you may decide to change some of it. Watch how your audience reacts – do they look scared during the spooky bits, and laugh when you want them to? Play with the volume and tone of your voice, until you get the reactions you hoped for.

## Find your listeners

Who did you write your story for? Girls like you, or little kids? Ask at school if you can tell your story to children of the right age group. Speak clearly and try not to gabble. See how much they enjoy it!

## Act together

Grab some pals to help you tell your story. Ask them to act out the adventure as you narrate it – perhaps they could take on the different character parts.

## Changed characters

If you're planning on performing to a big audience, find some costumes for yourself and your pals. If you can't find any good costumes, you could simply carry a different object for each part.

reporter

pirate

chef

maid

gardener

77

# Poetry princess

There are many kinds of poems. Some can make you laugh, while others are more serious. Poems often rhyme, but not always. See if you can write one yourself!

Poetry book

## Funny poems

Some poems are meant to make you laugh. They might be about silly things, or lines of complete nonsense filled with interesting, made-up words. Some poems raise a chuckle with clever rhymes or surprise the reader with daft endings.

## What's an acrostic?

Poems can be set out in all sorts of different ways. In an acrostic poem, the first letter of each line spells out a word. Can you write a poem like this, using all the letters of your name?

## Hear the beat

All poems have their own special rhythm. Lots of short words can speed up a poem, and longer words can slow it down. Not all poems rhyme, but all poems have a rhythm that you can clap out with your hands.

## A special kind of magic

If you want to write a poem, choose a subject that means a lot to you. It could be something happy or sad, or a message to someone you love. A poem is a very special, personal thing.

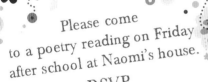

Please come to a poetry reading on Friday after school at Naomi's house.
RSVP
Yummy snacks and hot chocolate provided!

## Sensational!

Use all your senses when you write a poem – don't forget to describe sights, sounds, smells, tastes and sensations. Invent unusual comparisons to capture your reader's imagination.

## Be picky

When you write, choose every word with care. Creating a poem is almost like making music – each word has an effect on the sound and feel of the piece. If you run out of words that feel right, check out an online rhyming dictionary or thesaurus for inspiration.

# Drama queen

If you need a bit more drama in your life, don't wait to join a stage school. Play some of these brilliant acting games with your friends.

## Guess the advert

Split your friends into teams. Get each team to choose a product then act out an advert for it in under 30 seconds. The actor mustn't say what the advert is for – it's up to the team to guess correctly.

## Could you sell...?
- Shampoo
- Diamond rings
- Washing-up liquid
- Dog food
- Chewing gum

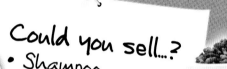

## Scene of the crime

Act out a crime scene news report with some pals. Decide who will be the reporter, police officer, witness and victim of the crime. Get someone to film your news piece, so that you can watch it back on TV.

## Impressive improv!

Acting without a script is called improvisation. Dig out some random objects from around the house, such as a mop or a funnel. Take turns with your friends to act out a funny scene, using one of these things as a prop.

## Pretend party

Choose someone to pretend to be a party host, with the rest of you playing guests. Each of the guests should have an amazing but secret profession, such as an astronaut, brain surgeon or champion dog trainer. During the scene the 'host' has to question the guests until she guesses each person's special job.

## Give us a clue

Pick a film, book or TV programme, then act out its title, word by word, without uttering a sound. The person who shouts out the title first gets the next turn.

## Feeling moody

Choose a word to describe a mood, such as 'excited', 'overjoyed' or 'cross'. A friend can ask you to perform something in that mood, like eating an apple. Can your friends guess what emotion you're trying to show?

# Play time

Were you born to perform? Do you dream of seeing your name up in lights one day? Kick-start your stage career by writing your own play, starring you and your friends of course!

## Get inspired

There are many different types of drama – from Christmas pantos to ancient Greek tragedies. Think about your favourite theatre trips or watch some plays on DVD to get your creative juices flowing.

## Every good script needs a...

- dramatic entrance
- touching moment
- funny joke
- cool heroine
- shocking surprise
- baddie to boo at

## Work together

If you're finding it tough to get started, try co-writing with a friend. Brainstorm together to see what you can come up with. Bounce off each other's ideas, inventing interesting plots and characters.

## Perfect parts

Count up how many friends want to be in your play so you can write parts for all of them. Try to give everyone a good-sized role, imagining what they might bring to each character.

## Setting the scene

Be realistic about the kind of show you can put on. It's better to produce a short piece really well than risk losing the audience's attention. Write a play that keeps the action in one place. It is difficult to make lots of different stage sets.

## Plot spot

The secret of a good plot is to keep it simple. Don't bring in too many story lines, but keep the action moving. You could adapt an old story, or invent a new one. Write in plenty of twists and turns to keep your audience gripped.

## Don't be a diva

If you work with a few friends on a play, there's bound to be the odd disagreement. Try to sort them out quickly and don't let anything get in the way of a great show! Make sure that even the quietest girl in the gang gets to have her say.

# Stage struck

You've finished writing your play – so what happens now? Cue rehearsals! Preparing for a production is lots of work, but you'll all feel very proud when the curtain goes up on opening night!

## Recruit your crew

Will you direct your play or would you prefer to be up on stage? You only need one director, but there are lots of other important jobs to do behind the scenes. If you're feeling shy, volunteer to sort out costumes or paint the set.

## Pick the cast

It's up to the director to choose who plays which part. If a part was written specially for someone, they should be given it. You may need to hold auditions for the rest of the cast, picking the people who give the best readings on the day.

DIRECTOR

## Learning lines

Everyone involved in the play will need a script. Type the play and print out copies for everyone to take home. Ask your friends to highlight their own lines on the script, and set a deadline for learning them.

## Go slowly

Once everyone has got to know their roles, start rehearsing together. Begin with a whole cast read-through, then split into groups to act out each of the scenes. Bring everyone together for a full dress rehearsal just before the big day.

## Pick a venue

The venue for your play is crucial. Maybe one of your friends has a big garden or front room that their parents will let you use. It might even be possible to get permission to perform your play at school.

## Director's job list

☆ plan the scenes
☆ tweak the script
☆ coach the actors
☆ practise the entrances and exits
☆ check the running time

## True professional

Fix a date for the performance and work towards it. Ask a pal or family member to be your prompter. Agree times for all the rehearsals so the right cast members turn up when they're needed.

85

# Look the part

Good stagecraft adds pizzazz to any performance. It's all about getting the costumes, make-up, props and sound effects right on the night!

## Hair affair

Practise all the hairstyles well before the final performance, so there are no last-minute disasters! To make a character's hair look right, you may need to use spray-on dye – always ask your parents first. If you want to wear wigs, browse in your local party shop.

## Costume drama

Ask at home if you can borrow clothes and props for your production. Get your friends to do the same. You may need to go to charity shops or car boot sales to pick up some bargains that will suit the characters you are playing.

## Magic make-up

Actors can't go on stage without make-up. Practise with some face paints, enhancing your features so that the audience can pick them out from a distance. Have fun, but don't overdo the colours!

## Curtain call

Check that there is space at the sides of your performing area for the cast to wait in between scenes. You could even decorate an old curtain to hang up at the front of the stage.

### Handy props

- telephone
- clock
- hat and scarf
- umbrella
- walking stick
- handbag
- camera

## Prop practice

Don't leave it too late to find or make props. You need time to rehearse with them. Remember not to use anything too fragile or precious as a prop, in case it gets broken or lost.

## Sounds good

Download sound effects and music onto your MP3, then burn them onto a CD. Put a friend in charge of the sound system so that she's ready to flick on the tracks at all the right times.

# On with the show!

You've put masses of time and energy into your play, now all you need is a good audience. Tell your friends and family about the show and spread the word about the hottest ticket in town!

## Poster publicity

Design a poster for your play. Don't forget to put on the title, plus the date, time and place! Stick your posters up well before the show so that no one misses out on your grand performance.

## Souvenir programme

Take some photos of your friends at the dress rehearsal and ask them to write a short paragraph about themselves. Make a play programme for the audience, adding the best photos next to each actor's biography. It will make a fantastic souvenir of the show.

### Programme checklist

- Title
- Writer's name
- Date of the performance
- Intro to the play
- Scenes
- Cast list
- Actor biogs
- Names of the backstage crew
- Special thank-yous

## Spread the word

Tell everyone you know about the show so that you play to a packed house. Ask your teachers if you can put a note in the school newsletter, too.

## Shine a light

Don't forget the lighting – perhaps your older brother or sister can help with this? A borrowed spotlight would add tons of drama to the performance. Practise using lights at the dress rehearsal first.

## Set the scene

Before the performance, put out enough seats for the audience, and print lots of programmes. Choose music to set the scene as the arrivals stream into the venue.

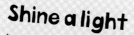

## Audience treat

Prepare snacks and drinks for the interval and for after the play. The cast could even bake muffins or cookies to bring on the night. A few sweet treats are sure to get your audience clapping!

# Star performer quiz

Are you a mega-star in waiting? Find out in this super showbiz quiz.

 **1.** How can you get better at singing?
- a   tell everyone how good you are
- b   watch pop videos
- c   practise singing every day

 **2.** How can you improve a song you have written?
- a   sing it to your pet
- b   video yourself singing then watch it back
- c   you can't, because it's perfect already

 **3.** If you want to invent a cool dance routine, you should:
- a   ask your dad for dance tips
- b   mix and match your steps to the mood of the music
- c   copy your favourite pop video

 **4.** What's the most important thing about talent contests?
- a   taking part
- b   showing off your skills
- c   winning a prize

 **5.** Good writers don't need to:
- a   plan the work
- b   make corrections
- c   worry about how good people think they are

 **6.** All the best poetry has to:
- a   be imaginative and creative
- b   rhyme
- c   be set out in verses

 **7.** What do actors do when they improvise?
- a   remember all their lines
- b   get stage fright
- c   act without reading from a script

 **8.** How can you put on the *best* performance of your play?
- a   leave everything to the last minute
- b   get organized well before the show
- c   don't worry – it will all be all right on the night

Look back at these pages: Sing up! (pages 64-65); Smash hit (pages 68-69); Dancing feet (pages 70-71); You've got talent! (pages 72-73); Tall tales (pages 74-75); Poetry princess (pages 78-79); Drama queen (pages 80-81); Stage struck (pages 84-85); Look the part (pages 86-87).

## How well did you do? Count your correct answers below to find out!

**0-3**   You've got bags of confidence, but there's more to learn about getting your act just right. Don't give up – you'll be an accomplished performer in no time!

**4-6**   Not bad! You know what you're good at, and what you need to do to improve your skills. Keep going – you've got real talent!

**7-8**   Congratulations! If you carry on like this you'll be famous one day. Your charisma and creativity are infectious!

Quiz answers: 1. c, 2. b, 3. b, 4. a, 5. c, 6. a, 7. c, 8. b.

Happy and Healthy

# Get fit!

You only have one body – so it's up to you to look after it. Getting active is the best way to keep yourself happy and healthy. Just go for it!

## Couch potato

Do you watch too much TV? Make a note every day of how long you sit in front of the telly. After a week, look back at how many hours you spent – is it time to cut back and do something more active instead?

## Computer crazy?

Surfing the web and playing computer games don't give your muscles much of a workout! Take regular breaks and listen to your mum or dad if they nag you to jump up and do something else!

## Take it outside!

Fix a time to meet your friends after school – why not use up some energy skating around the park or shooting hoops at the local basketball court? Don't forget to tell someone at home where you're going and when you'll be back.

## Stretch your legs

Look for new ways to make exercise part of your everyday life. If you have an older brother or sister, ask them to walk to school with you instead of getting a lift. If you live too far away, ask your parents to park the car nearby and stride the last part of the journey.

## Brilliant biking

Cycling is a super-quick way to get about! If you are not confident at riding yet, go out with your mum or dad a few times first. Always wear a helmet and choose routes that are safe for cycling.

## Road safety

If you are walking with friends or riding on your bikes, take care near busy roads. If you are cycling, wear a helmet and make sure that you can be easily seen in the dark.

## Move it!
why not...?
- scooter to the shops
- jog round the block
- ban lifts and take the stairs
- power-walk the dog
- skateboard down the street

# Indoor play

Weather not so good? There are still hundreds of indoor sports you can enjoy! Get ready to challenge yourself and share lots of giggles at the same time...

## Get together

If you are shy and find it hard to make friends, join a sports club. There are clubs all over the country for every sport you can think of. You could even have some lessons first to help build your confidence.

## Fantastic gymnastics

Gymnastics is a cool indoor sport for girls. You can go to gym classes, and there are lots of badges and awards to work for as you improve your skills.

## Sky-high

Trampolining keeps you fit and uses up loads of energy. The trick to good bouncing is to get into a rhythm! Learn some awesome moves, then make up your own routine.

## Gym basics

Can you crack all six?
1. forward roll
2. handstand
3. backward roll
4. cartwheel
5. headstand
6. hand spring

## Super skating

Ice-skating is an Olympic sport that can be really competitive. It takes years of hard work to become an ice-skating champ, but there's lots of fun to be had just gliding around your local rink!

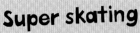

## Dance studio

Moving to music will have you working up a sweat in no time! There are so many ways to do it too. Ballet, tap, jazz, street, Latin and ballroom are all different kinds of dancing.

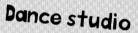

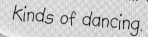

## Watch out!

Martial arts such as judo, ju-jitsu and karate can help keep you both fit and safe. The skills you learn are handy for self-defence. One of the first things you will be taught is how to tumble without hurting yourself.

# Splash time

If you can't swim, take the plunge and learn! If you're already pool-confident, work on improving your strokes so that you speed up in the water.

## Splashing sports
Give these wicked water sports a try!
- surfing
- canoeing
- waterskiing
- snorkelling
- windsurfing
- rowing

## Water baby
Don't worry if all your mates can swim, but you can't. It's never too late to learn! Sign up for beginner's lessons. Some pools even run crash courses to get you swimming quickly.

## Choose life
If you can swim already and want a new challenge, why not learn to be a junior life-saver? You learn about water safety, life-saving and how to deal with emergencies.

## Keep keen
If you want to race in swimming galas, you'll have to practise hard, but it's well worth the effort! Training usually starts early in the morning, before the school day begins.

## Dive in!

If you get a real buzz from diving, it's worth finding a teacher to help you develop your technique. Always check that the water is deep enough to allow you to dive safely.

## At sea

If you swim in the sea, make sure you go with an adult. There are currents and waves that could carry even strong swimmers away from the shore. Look out for and obey warning flags too – they are there to keep you safe.

## Pool party

There's so much fun to be had at your local leisure centre! Find out if your pool runs Saturday splash-time sessions, work out in a water aerobics class or make up a synchro swimming routine with your friends.

# Outdoor action

Playing sport in the open air works your muscles and gets your heart rate jumping! Winning is also a fab feeling, but nothing beats being part of a great team.

## Footie mad

In the UK, more girls play football than netball. So why not join your nearest football club? Be prepared to get muddy when you play!

## Anyone for tennis?

Tennis may not be an obvious team game, but if you join a tennis club, you'll make loads of new friends. Doubles matches are always good fun – especially if it's a close game!

## Old favourites

Do you play handball, hockey or netball at school? These are all brilliant team sports. When you train, you'll learn tactics and you'll improve your co-ordination.

## Sophie's Annual Garden Games

### Starts 2.00pm, next Saturday

**Events:** limbo dancing

wheelbarrow racing

toss the welly

assault course

## Medal dreams

Can you run faster than your friends, jump higher or throw a ball further across the park? Athletics may be for you! Start training now for a gold medal at the next Olympics, or set up a mini-Games in your back garden.

## On the map

Orienteering is an outdoor activity that gives you tons of fresh air and exercise. You and your pals use a map and compass to find a set of marked spots, before racing back to base. Give it a go!

## Work it out

If sport is not your thing, don't say no to all outdoor exercise – just be creative about it! You could try setting up a treasure hunt so you and your pals can run around to find the clues.

# Eat smart

You're more likely to keep fit and well if you have a nutritious diet. This means eating healthy meals, saving sweets and treats for special occasions.

## Meal deal

You may be a busy bee, but find time to eat three meals a day. Don't skip breakfast, or munch too much between meal times. If you must have a snack, make healthy choices.

## Balancing act

There are five key food groups. You should eat some food from each group during the day, eats lots of 1 and 2 and only a little of 4.

1. breads and cereals
2. fruit and vegetables
3. dairy foods
4. sweet and fatty foods
5. meat, fish and eggs

## Five a day

Fruit and vegetables are stuffed full of vitamins and minerals which all help your body to work properly. Make a big effort to eat five portions of fruit and vegetables every single day.

## Eat up!

Don't forget that smoothies and fruit juice count towards your five-a-day. Don't try to hide the salad and veggies on your plate – eat them all up, including the greens!

## Dairy foods

Creamy dairy foods like yoghurt, milk and cheese have calcium in them – a mineral that helps your bones and teeth be strong. Be dairy food-friendly and drink milky drinks whenever you can.

## Feeling thirsty?

We all need to eat food, but water is even more important for our survival. You need to drink at least one or two litres of water a day – even more if the weather is hot.

# Snack and go

Next time you take sandwiches to school or go on a picnic, pack some new things in your lunchbox! There are all sorts of tasty dips, wraps and snacks to try.

## Brown is best

Brown bread is better for you than white bread, because it contains wholemeal grains. Get used to eating brown bread in your sandwiches – and try to eat the crusts, too!

## Pack a snack

Next time you're packing for a picnic, ask your mum or dad if you can leave any unhealthy stuff at home. Replace crisps and chocolate with options like fruit, cereal bars and nuts.

## DIY nibbles

Ask if you can bake your own yummy treats. Flapjacks taste great and they are good for you too! If you make too many to eat by yourself, take some into school to share with your pals. There's a tasty flapjack recipe on page 104.

## Mix it up

Always take a bottle of water out with you – it's important to top up your fluid levels throughout the day. If you're tired of plain tap water, add a dash of fruit juice to give it some flavour.

### This week's sandwiches

| | |
|---|---|
| Monday | cream cheese, ham and cucumber |
| Tuesday | tuna crunch |
| Wednesday | houmous and grated carrot |
| Thursday | chicken, chutney and spinach |
| Friday | prawn mayonnaise |

## Plan ahead

You'll soon get bored if you always eat the same thing. Experiment with different fillings for your sandwiches, rolls and wraps. Plan a week's lunches, so you eat something different every day.

### Shopping list
tin of tuna
baby spinach
red pepper
cream cheese
tortilla wraps

## Get involved

Make a list of the healthy snacks that you would like to eat when you're on the go. Talk about the list with your mum and dad, then go shopping together to buy the tasty things you're after.

# Get cooking

The best way to learn to cook is to get in the kitchen and help! Watch how your mum or dad prepare food, then pull on an apron and join in.

## Baking flapjacks

Make a batch of fruity flapjacks. These scrummy snacks aren't just delicious, they're healthy, too!

### Super-quick flapjacks

You will need:

125g margarine
100g soft dark-brown sugar
60g golden syrup
225g porridge oats
75g dried fruit or nuts*

*Why not add dried sultanas, apricots, coconut or a mix of nuts and seeds?

1. Set the oven to 180°C/350°F/ Gas Mark 4.
2. Ask an adult to help you melt the margarine, sugar and golden syrup in a non-stick saucepan.
3. Stir in the oats and dried fruit.
4. Scrape the mixture into a baking tin, then pop it in the oven for half an hour.
5. Take out, let cool and cut into slices!

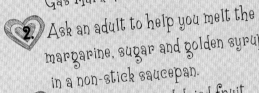

## Cupcake creations

For a special occasion, have a go at baking some cupcakes. When they're cool, whip up some buttercream icing, then sprinkle your cakes with pretty decorations.

## Make a menu

When you've had some practice in the kitchen, try cooking a complete meal. Get together with a friend and plan a starter, main course and dessert. Keep things simple the first time around.

Take care in the kitchen. Always ask a grown-up to help you before chopping food or using the oven or hob.

## Get organized

Write a list of all the ingredients that you'll need for your meal. Go shopping to buy the stuff, then get cooking!

## Dine in style

To make your meal extra special, decorate the kitchen like a posh restaurant, with flowers, napkins and a tablecloth. Write out the menu, so your guests know what dishes to look forward to!

# Looking good

It's important to try to look your best, because looking good also makes you feel great. Find your style and get ready to shine!

### New style
With long hair, there are all sorts of styles you can try out, but girls with short hair can have fun too! If you have a shorter cut, jazz up your look with clips, gels and funky hair accessories.

### Twisty buns
Always brush your hair before you style it to tug out the tangles! Give boring old bunches a makeover by twisting them into messy buns. Try fixing a side bun, or even two high ones at the back.

### Plait trick
Wash your hair and tie it into lots of little plaits while it is damp. Leave your hair to dry naturally, then untie the plaits. You'll be left with tumbling, wavy hair!

## Fashion exchange

If you're fed up with your wardrobe, don't wait until your next shopping trip. Ask your mum or dad, then revamp your style by swapping clothes with your best friend.

## Fashionista wardrobe tips

★ organize clothes by colour
★ keep your shoes neatly in a rack
★ give to charity anything you haven't worn for a year
★ pop a fragranced cushion in with socks, tights and pjs

## Makeovers and make-up

It is fun to experiment with make-up, but try not to overdo it when you give your friend a makeover! Just a dab of lip gloss and a touch of blusher will give her a lovely, natural look.

## Attention to detail

Looking good is all about the details. Pick accessories that make the most of your clothes. Break up boring tops with a funky belt or team with a sparkly necklace.

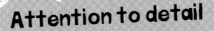

# Perfectly polished

Looking good isn't just about fashion – it's about taking care of your whole body, inside and out!

## Choose your treats

Did you know that the good eating habits explained earlier can also affect your looks? If you want glowing skin and lovely hair, say 'no' to junk food. When you are hungry, choose fruit instead of crisps, and water instead of fizzy drinks.

## Wonderful water

Your skin needs lots and lots of water! Drink plenty to keep it feeling soft. Wash your face in lukewarm water every morning and evening, using a clean towel to gently pat the skin dry.

## Sun and sleep

Your skin is precious, so look after it well. Get enough beauty sleep every night – if you don't feel fresh, your skin won't look fresh! In hot weather, use sun block and wear a sun hat to protect your skin.

## Hair food

A good diet will help to keep your hair shiny and healthy too. Foods like meat, fish, cheese and eggs are full of protein – just the stuff for glossy, shiny hair.

## Good hair day

Be kind to your hair! Brush it well every day, and have regular trims at the hairdresser's. This will stop you getting split ends and keep your hair in tip-top condition.

## Salon secrets

1. Wash your hair regularly.
2. Always rinse your locks after swimming.
3. When you wash your hair, let it dry naturally sometimes.
4. If you have to use a hairdryer, dry your hair with a towel first.
5. Don't brush your hair when it's wet or it might stretch and break.

# Freshen up

Do you like chilling out at the end of the day in a lovely hot bath? Care for your body from top to toe and let your natural beauty shine through!

## Smelly stuff

Water is best for your skin when you bathe or shower – you don't need loads of soaps and products, however sweet they smell. Warm water will clean out tiny pores in your skin without blocking them up.

## Sensitive skin

If you are muddy after playing outside, then you'll need to use some soap to get the dirt off! If your skin is sensitive, choose a mild soap and don't use too much of it.

## Break a sweat

When you do something energetic, such as your favourite sport, you may get a bit sweaty. This doesn't have to be a problem – just put on some deodorant before you go out.

110

## Handy hygiene

It's important to wash your hands during the day, especially before you eat, after going to the toilet and when you've played with your pet. Washing your hands stops germs from spreading.

## Love those nails!

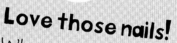

When you have a bath or shower, check your hands and clean your fingernails if you need to! Long, dirty fingernails don't look great, so try to file them so they stay neat.

## Brush up

No one likes smelly breath, so make sure you don't have it. Clean your teeth every morning after breakfast, and every evening before bedtime. Have regular check-ups at the dentist too.

## Prepare to impress

Make time to get ready for special occasions.

- 1 hour before: take a bubbly bath
- 45 minutes before: dry your hair
- 30 minutes before: get dressed
- 20 minutes before: style or pin up hair
- 10 minutes before: add a touch of make-up
- 5 minutes before: spritz on your favourite perfume

# Feeling good

Feeling happy helps you stay healthy. Even when you're super-busy with school and friends, try to make time to de-stress and unwind.

## Don't worry!

Try not to worry too much. Worrying makes you sad and it can stop you sleeping well at night. When you're tired, you are more likely to catch a cold or get ill.

## Talk about it

If something is bugging you, don't keep it a secret. Talking to someone will make you feel heaps better. Sharing a problem is the first step towards sorting it out.

## Get some help

If a problem won't go away, talk to an adult you trust, for example your teacher or someone in your family. If you are being bullied, this person will be able to help you get things straightened out.

## Stop the stress

If you are feeling stressed, stop what you are doing and do something else that you really enjoy. Play some sport or music, or make a fuss of your pet!

## Wind down

We all need plenty of sleep so that we can grow and function properly. If you find it hard to doze off at night, make sure you unwind before you go to bed.

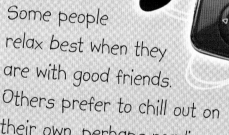

## Just relax!

Some people relax best when they are with good friends. Others prefer to chill out on their own, perhaps reading quietly or listening to music. How do you relax?

## Stress busters!

☺ take five deep breaths
☺ phone a caring friend
☺ take a long walk
☺ think of all your favourite things
☺ hug someone you love

# Spoil yourself

'Me time' matters! If you don't stop and spoil yourself sometimes, you'll end up feeling worn out and fed up.

## Get pampered

Make a date with your mates to have a girly pampering session. Try out some new make-up, paint your nails and do some homemade beauty treatments! Relax and have a good laugh together.

Sunita is invited to **Katie's** bedroom spa pampering session on Friday after school

Please bring your dressing gown and a hair brush

RSVP [No little brothers allowed!]

## Cool as a cucumber

After a long day at school, lie on the sofa and shut your eyes. Rest a thin slice of cucumber on each eyelid – it's a great way to soothe and refresh your tired eyes.

## Shop till you drop

If you really need cheering up, the only answer may be to hit the shops with a friend. Treat yourselves to a cake in a café, then blow your pocket money on something you've had your eye on for ages!

## Happy faces

Give your best mate a facial massage. Smooth her forehead and cheeks with your fingertips, working in small circles. Be very gentle and try not to tickle!

## Smells good

Are you bored with the bottle of perfume you got last birthday? Have a scent-swapping party – the best bit is trying out the perfumes and deciding which one you like best!

## One-to-one

Ask your mum or dad to take you out somewhere, just the two of you. It doesn't have to be an expensive outing – you'll have fun being together, and doing something different for a change.

# sleep tight

Everyone needs to sleep – even dynamic divas like you! Your body is growing, and that takes up loads of vital energy.

## A good night's sleep

If you don't get enough sleep, you can become tired and grumpy. You might also find it difficult to work properly at school. You need about ten hours of sleep a night to stay healthy and happy.

## Early night

It sounds obvious, but the easiest way to get more sleep is to go to bed earlier! On school days try to be an early bird, saving your late nights for the weekend.

## Calm down

Choose to do calming things just before bedtime. Have a nice bath, and have a hot, milky drink. Don't do anything that makes your brain or body have to work too hard!

## One last thing

Sometimes it's hard to get to sleep, but there can be good reasons for this. Give yourself time to wind down before you go to bed – don't play computer games or watch loud TV shows just before you turn out the light.

## Bedtime story

Try to get into the habit of reading a relaxing book at bedtime. It can be a novel, short story or even one of your school subjects! You could listen to a talking book CD. You'll soon feel sleepy and ready to drop off.

## Off to sleep

If you really can't get to sleep, stop worrying. That will only keep you awake longer. Instead, think about something completely different – like an A to Z list of all your favourite celebs!

## Dreamer's dictionary

**chocolate** time for a treat
**forest** think something through
**letter** listen to your heart
**party** be more sociable
**tunnel** keep moving forwards

# Happy and healthy quiz

Are you healthy inside and out? Find out the answer to this great lifestyle quiz.

1. What's the healthiest way to get to school?
   a share a lift
   b walk or cycle
   c take the bus

2. Which of these indoor sports will teach you to be fit and safe?
   a judo
   b chess
   c gymnastics

3. What's the best way to get into a new sport?
   a watch people playing it on telly
   b wait until a friend is interested too
   c sign yourself up at your local sports club

4. Which girls' sport is even more popular than netball?
   a football
   b hockey
   c tennis

5. Which of these meals is it OK to miss?
   a breakfast
   b any meal, if you don't fancy it
   c you should never miss a meal

6. Which of these helps your skin?
   a fizzy drinks
   b junk food
   c water

7. If you're stressed, what's a good way to unwind?
   a play a computer game
   b take a long walk
   c eat a takeaway

8. How much sleep do you really need?
   a as little as you can get away with
   b about six hours a night
   c about ten hours a night

Look back at these pages: *Get fit!* (pages 92-93); *Indoor play* (pages 94-95); *Outdoor action* (pages 98-99); *Eat smart* (pages 100-101); *Perfectly polished* (pages 108-109); *Feeling good* (pages 112-113); *Sleep tight* (pages 116-117).

## How well did you do? Count your correct answers below to find out!

0-3  You're on the right track, but there's stacks more you can learn about how to stay happy and healthy.

4-6  Not bad! You've got a pretty clear idea of what's good for you and what isn't! Keep up the great work.

7-8  You're the best! You know what to do to make sure you always look and feel amazing.

Quiz answers: 1. b, 2. a, 3. c, 4. a, 5. c, 6. c, 7. b, 8. c

# Index